The Little Book for BIG Change

How to get out of your way

and

Create a life of ease, joy and creativity!

by

Purim King, LCSW

D1512114

King & Princess Publishing

San Francisco ◆ New York

The Little Book For BIG Change.

Copyright© 2014 by Core Wellness

Library of Congress Control Number: 2014948356

ISBN-10: 1500793167

ISBN-13: 978-1500793166

Front Cover Design by Adelle King

First Printing, 2014

Printed in the United States of America

Published by
King & Princess Publishing
450 23rd Ave, Suite 1
San Francisco, CA 94121

To
Meatboy
with love
Purim
914-417-1924

DEDICATION

I dedicate this book in loving memory.

To my mother, Rosa.

Also to my father, Moshe.

CONTENTS

FORWARD

Purim and I have enjoyed the adventure of our friendship for almost twenty years. We have travelled together to learn with master teachers; we have taken paths together, where we explored reality, spirituality, grew as parents, expanded our relationships; and now we have become teachers and elders. Our world needs teachers and elders to share their knowledge and wisdom so all of us can move toward our greater fulfillment as human beings.

This book is a collection of some of the tools in her magic bag from a lifetime of experience that makes a true master. She is a master because over her lifetime, she has dared to be a mystic, a psychic, a spiritual advisor, an intuitive, a healer. All of her roles in these alternative fields, offer the world another chance to function more humanely, more effectively and more consciously.

Purim has always asked me the questions that helped me to follow the higher path and she has always been my gifted advisor. When we have worked together, I am in awe of Purim's ability to craft her words to create the most effective solution for each individual… whether it was me, one of her clients, or one of her students.

This book is only a portion of her gifted insight into human nature and psychological wellbeing. I look forward to many more publications that share her methods for big change inside a little book. Don't be deceived by the title or this initial message, because inside this book is a huge program to begin your life of richness, ease, wholeness, courage and freedom. Yes, freedom. You are free to have an amazing life.

- Bari Falese, Reverend, Artist, Poet/Writer, Conservator, Survivalist and Multicultural Shaman

Purim King, LCSW

ACKNOWLEDGMENTS

I'm grateful to you, my client and reader, for entrusting me with your life challenges and stories and allowing me to be a small contribution to you and to the world.

I'm grateful to my teachers: Trudy, Dr. Barbara Ann Brennan, Ron Kurtz, Dr. Greg Johansson, Garry Douglas and Dr. Dain Heer, and many others.

A special gratitude to Adelle King, my daughter, for her amazing contribution to my life and to this book.

I'm forever grateful to Bari Falese for her encouragement, for her editorial contributions and friendship. This book may mot have come to be without her input, insight and patience.

I would also like to acknowledge my sister, Carolina Kagan, and long-time friend, Francoise Borrel, for their support, belief in me and loving friendship..

Lastly, while not directly involved in the birth of "The little book for BIG change" my husband and my son are a driving force in my life and I'm grateful for them.

Purim King, LCSW

1

MY STORY

I was the sick person and the black sheep in my family. From the age of 20 days old, I had a bad skin disorder, and from 3 years of age, I had developed a very bad asthma. It was the asthma that brought me in and out of hospitals.

I remember feeling better as soon as I arrived in the hospital, even before the doctor or the nurse saw me or gave me any treatment. And yet, even then, I did not trust doctors. I was aware that they did not have the answer to my disease and that they were guessing at what treatment to use. I was their guinea pig. Sometimes I cooperated with the medications and prescriptions and sometime I flushed the meds down the toilets. I and other kids, too.

I was about six or seven years old and back in the hospital. I was familiar with the staff in the hospital and even with some of the other patients. We, the regulars, knew a lot about our caregivers. Sometimes news flew so quickly; we believed we knew more about them then they knew about us. A new doctor came to our unit. She was there for a short time, but that was all I needed. She walked with a cane and we whispered that she had polio as a child, but that was not what made her stand out. She took time with us, somehow she could relate to us in a way the rest of the staff didn't. I don't know if I consciously understood and articulated all that then, but all of a sudden I knew who and what I wanted to be! I told any one willing to hear me:

One day I'll be a doctor, but not like them! One day I'll be a doctor, but not like them!

I did not stop to think what exactly does this mean *"a doctor, but not like them?"* I believed I would go to medical school. For the next thirteen years or so I worked towards that goal. I took advanced biology, chemistry and math in high school. I took summer jobs in nursing homes and provided direct care to a paralyzed woman suffering from MS.I applied to the medical department of one university, the Jerusalem University. That was the most competitive and difficult program to get in to in my environment and I didn't get in. Many of my friends became medical doctors or dentists. Some traveled to Italy to complete the first three years and transferred back to Israel, some started with biology, some went to dental school. As far as I know, I was the only one among my friends that did not go to medical school after all. I went to accounting school. When I put accounting as my second choice I never considered it as an option, it was so foreign to me.

From where I stand today it all makes so much sense. But at twenty it created confusion. I could not pass statistics and felt like a failure, fully knowing that it was my attention, not my mental capacity that was the problem. I dropped out of college and became an insurance agent. I loved the interaction with people, and the teaching that a sale involved. I was good, but it was not it. I started a search for "IT", for my passion. I took a class in advertising, I studied television and production, took a painting class or two. I worked more or less in each of those fields and I do love the creative aspect of both advertising and television, but it was not the "IT" I was searching for.

A husband, two children, a new country, many sales jobs and much pain later, at the age of forty plus, I heard a story about a healer, somewhere in South America, who would put his hands on people and transform them, in a moment. My heart skipped a beat and I felt a deep longing to be like that healer. While not much changed in the outside appearance of my world, that was the precise moment my journey home began. The journey from where I stood to who I am.

My hope in telling my story is that it may be that spark which will awaken your longing, create clarity, remind you of *"who you are"*.

For years I was missing something, feeling empty and trying to fill in that emptiness with things and more things. Looking back, many times people would cross my path and quietly point to my passion, my path. Even before I applied to college, my client the MS patient who was a retired head-nurse from a major hospital repeatedly advised me to become a nurse, not a doctor. When I was in sales, my superiors and my friends would tease me and say that I should be a social worker, because I would care more about helping the client than making a sale. People in need would find their way to me, asking for help, always benefiting from their interaction with me.

6

I considered both nursing and social work in my youth, but my ego stood in the way. It may be that I needed the search! I learned many valuable skills during those years. Still the thought that I may have gone trough life, never discovering my passion, not becoming *me*, creates instant sadness and pain. Those feelings are now replaced with a deep sense of gratitude, peace and appreciation of the abundant opportunities and freedoms I had and have. Today I'm happy with me, I like who I am. I used to fear that if you knew me you might not like me anymore. Today I know that to know me is to love me, and if you choose not to get to know me, we both lose.

Here are two slogans that have helped me move out of the wilderness and the fear:

You can't get enough of what you do not want! If it's yours you can't loose it; if it is not yours, you can't hold onto it!

This has been my story. I share it in the hopes that it and the tools in this book will inspire you to find and create your own story and to finding, having and loving you!

2

WHY DO WE NEED ANOTHER BOOK?

The answer to why we need another book is because we all hear and process information differently. Spirit moves me to write. I hope spirit moves some of you to read this little book, practice some of the insights within it, and have a more fun life.

This small book started with my desire to share my "DIRTY" words with you. Dirty words that I ask you to consider eliminating from your vocabulary. Those are not the F and S words! Swearing helps one to express bottled-up anger. It's not the best way to express oneself, but still helpful to a degree. The words I'll share with you are way sneakier. They play tricks on us; influence our attitude, willingness, and outcomes, and not for the better. As I progressed with the writing, this book evolved into a tool kit for life.

Since 1996, I've worked as a psychic reader in a fair where I see about 20 or more people a day for eight weekends during the summers. I use the reading to find out the major issue the person in front of me is dealing with at the time. I then coach them on how to create a positive change in their life. This book is summation of the advice I have given over and over to these folks. Some listen and some don't. Those who follow my advise and take action often come back to tell me the ways their lives have changed, as if by magic. My readings, as is this book, are not intended to provide in-depth therapy or counseling. Still, using just one of the topics that follow, my clients' lives have expanded. They report completing tasks that had eluded them for some time, getting a good partner, or simply moving smoothly forward. I frankly believe that the information I share with you here would benefit us all, if we'd simply learned it in school. It is elementary.

This book is not about becoming a linguistic expert or embarking on a long course of study. It is more like a daily practice for sanity. I'm inviting you to have an awareness of how what you say and think affects you and your behavior. I believe in the power of a story to illustrate a point and make it memorable. When I tell a story, whether it's about me or something else, it is for emphasis and the ease of grasping the concept I'm talking about. The accuracy of the story is not important. With that said, people lose track of the important information and get lost in pile of words and repetitions. So, a small book it is! I'm keeping it concise on purpose. As to the big change, that is up to you. The best pill will not heal you unless you swallow it! Use these tools and make them your own. This book is an invitation to grow, expand, and to be more of you.

I'm writing here as if the information comes from my experience and it does, but it is not a new discovery. It is not mine for the most part. I've read many books and heard some of this from different sources. I could write it as an academic paper with references and quotes, but I find that annoying to read. I chose to write it as if you and I are sitting and talking to each other.

I find that many of us, much of the time, do not know what we feel, think, and how we behave. When I started my journey, I had one emotion—sadness. I had anger that I would not see or admit to. I was lying to myself all the time. It took the awareness of a friend for me to hear the demeaning words of my partner and those I said to myself. We have two ears, but we do not hear what others say or even what we say. Yet other times, we hear things, real or imagined, and for whatever reason, we choose to believe or resist them. With that, we create a belief system that holds those patterns in place and colors our experience of our world: how we see the world and other people, how we see our self in the world, and what is possible and impossible for us.

When we suppress our feelings for a very long time, it may seem that, if we let ourselves feel our emotions, we will drown in them. But what if we are bigger than the anger and the sadness? As a small child, it may have been a good idea to keep the anger to oneself. Is it true today as an adult? How much does denying our emotions cost us? Is there an appropriate way to feel our feelings without creating conflict? When I finally got in touch with my sadness, for a moment it felt enormous. I was just a river of endless tears. I sobbed for three months straight, and then it was over and a weight was lifted from me. It takes courage to walk this way. It takes willingness to look at those places we deem too scary, uncomfortable, and embarrassing about our person. The journey is to discover the parts of us that we hide from ourselves. So, if you are not up to knowing the truth, close this book and throw it away!

If you choose to stay, give your self a break. It took years of therapy and schooling to have the awareness I have today. And, by God, I'm not close to done. Be patient with yourself and acknowledge your own courage to hear the call of your soul and answer it. We all work hard to hide our power, talents, and longing to express and be. Looking at those aspects, we judge most about our self can be scary and also very rewarding.

Awareness of how I feel, how I talk to myself, and what I choose to believe or not, has given me the ability to accomplish many feats that I used to believe I was incapable of. It made it possible for me to sing in front of an audience, paint and have my work sell, complete both my Bachelor's and Master's degrees in less then 3 years while working and being a mom and a wife, and finally embark upon writing this book, to name some. I'm not bragging. I may never be a name artist or be considered a famous writer for that matter. But using my talents and contributing to others even just a little, is what makes my life full and joyful. This is what makes me feel good to be me. That is what, for me, makes the journey worth the effort.

We can walk in this world in pain, fear, and anger, or we can walk in peace and joy. <u>It is a choice!</u> I invite you to read on and I hope to be a contribution to you finding peace and joy in your life. Like a spring on the side of the road, may this work resource you.

This book is intended to give you some of the shortcuts I've learned. "Successful" people would say: "All I needed to do is get out of my way!" It used to infuriate me, because no one actually tells you how to do that. How do I get out of my way? The insights I will share with you are some of the how-to get out of your way. It is not a standalone magic wand that will drop millions of dollars in your lap, get you the prince or princess you've dreamed of, make your family magically change to the Brady Bunch, or some other fantasy. What I hope to give you is more like a shovel that you can use to clear the snow or level the ditch you are in so you can get out on the road to your destination; destination not as a place to arrive to, but more as a direction for the journey of your life.

One way I use some of the books I have is to open them randomly and consider the information on the page as guidance for the day. It always amazes me how relevant the text is to what is going on in my life at the time. My motto is: If you feel alone or stuck, just open a book. <u>When stuck, you often require more information</u>. This book seams to be a good device for daily guidance. Another way is to read the whole book through, and then choose one chapter and play with it for a month. When you own that tool and you've practiced it until it is second nature to you, move on to another chapter.

Have fun!

If you like this little book and it's made its contribution to you, consider sharing it with others. If this little book does not talk to you right now, that's OK. I have books that sit at the side of my bed for years before I'm ready for them. And then there are books that literally knock me on the head. And still, there are those that leave and come back later. If this one came to you, it is for you. However, if it is not right for you at this moment, give it away! The information you require will find you in just the right time. Did you know: <u>you can't lose what is yours, and you can't hang on to what is not yours?</u>

Another slogan that I like and that is appropriate here is: <u>When the student is ready, the teacher will show up.</u> That is how I experience the world. A teacher, as intended here, is not necessarily a scholar or a professor. A teacher could be an annoying coworker, an accident, or a sentence on TV or on a billboard. It is anything that grabs your attention and brings more awareness in you. It can be this book.

Ready? Let the journey home to you begin! Discovering, befriending, and knowing yourself is the ultimate journey we all take. Like in the movie "Groundhog Day", it may take several tries before we get there, but we all get there, and then we keep on going. What can be more fun than this?

PART I

3

KNOWING

I talk of <u>knowing as a sense</u>, like seeing. Use your mind to consciously ask for information or awareness; the answer comes not from your head and/or from thinking. It comes like an "aha-moment"; a knowing. It is factual information. Knowing has a sense of truth to it and needs no explanation. Sometimes it is as a remembering of something long forgotten, or something you were aware of and just now are able to connect it to the question at hand.

I used to have a dream journal. I would write a question and then record the dreams that followed. At first I could not find any connection (God was not talking to me and neither were my dreams). Then one day, with some distance of time, I read the journal again and it was amazing: I had knowing: question-answer, question-answer. What was even more amazing was that the answers were relevant to this moment now and the information was what I needed to have in order to move on at the present. Don't discount something just because you can't see it now.

<u>Knowing is a sense!</u>

<u>Waiting for a knowing is not a passive state, it is more like looking for a misplaced object. You don't know where it is, and maybe you don't know what exactly it looks like, but when you find it, you know you got it.</u>

On a different level, <u>knowing is action.</u> When I say "I know smoking is bad for me" and I continue to smoke, do I really know? For if I really got it that this cigarette I'm about to light is the one that will give me my final and everlasting ticket to my maker, unless I'm suicidal, I probably would not smoke it. When I say that I know smoking is bad for me, I'm saying that I buy into the belief system that it has negative effect on the body. I agree

15

that some people may get cancer as result of smoking, may be even me, but not today. Today, I'm fine and I like to enjoy my cigarette, if you don't mind. <u>Knowing, in this sense, requires change in direction, a new and different action.</u>

In the smoking example, I'm saying: I'm OK with killing myself, but when my throat hurts, I go to the doctor and act as if I like to be in this world. In a way, there is a <u>contradiction</u> within me: like to live vs. like to die.

We do this with relationships, with money, jobs, and so on. This is one of the reasons we get stuck. Contradictions create two even forces facing each other; <u>it is me vs. me = stuck.</u>

<u>Knowing something requires different and congruent action. It is one way effort I choose to live, so I take care of my body, mind and soul.</u>

4

TRUTH

Light or Heavy

The body is our record keeper and our Jiminy Cricket. It tells us when we are off course and it tells us when we are in integrity with ourselves. It has no capacity to lie. It talks in sensations. When we are off-course, it gives us a small pain. When we listen and change, the pain goes away and we are back to health. If we choose to ignore the body's signals, over time we get sick; we get an acute or a chronic disease. Disease can be physical or emotional or mental. Dis-ease can be a difficulty with employment, or relationships or making decisions and so on.

I just want to say that there is no negative intent or weakness of character, or blame here. There are many reasons people get sick or hurt that go beyond the scope of this book. The point is that we have power to change, that which no longer serves us.

Check out for yourself:

If you say: I'm the victim of this economy. How do you feel? Did your body relax and feel light, big and expanded or did it contract and tighten up, feeling small and heavy? It feels heavy. It is not true.

And if you say: I'm the creator of the world! How does you body feel? It is light and calm, right. You sort of stand a bit taller, expanded. This is a truth.

I will ask you to check with your body for light or heavy. Sometimes my truth may be that walking in the rain is fun, while your truth may be that walking in the rain is not a good idea. We will get different readings. And some times, say, drinking a soft drink today is not good for my body, but when I ask next time it is beneficial.

When I say true for you, I mean it is congruent with your best interest and that of all others. You can ask this about any action or decision you make: Is this congruent with my best interest? Will it be a contribution to me 5 years from now? The projection into the future helps you not to be too attached to a particular outcome in this moment.

Here is the truth about truth: it needs no explanation, or justification. When you are explaining, you are lying, mostly to your self. This hint has been very valuable tool for me. Honesty with oneself is needed before we can search for "THE TRUTH".

If, say, I come late to an appointment – the truth is, I'm late. Everything I may tell you or try to tell myself as to why I'm late is irrelevant. It is best to apologize for being late and not tell a story about traffic and so on, even if there was heavy traffic. The truth is that I'm late and if I cared to be on time I would have been. Making justifications is insulting to people's intelligence.

The point is to be willing to know the truth, even when it is not pretty. Ask for the truth, and search or wait for the answer. It is not in your head. Getting clear awareness of the truth will become easy with practice.

5

IN GOD'S IMAGE

The Bible tells us that man was created in the image of GOD. Think about it. What is the one function we know God has? He creates – the world, the people, the animals, and so on. And man and women are created in his image. He is the creator, and we are creators, too. This is our main function.

God creates and sometimes he destroys his creations. And so do we. We create and we destroy our creations. Only God can destroy God's creation; man can destroy man's creation, but not Gods creation. We create thoughts, emotions, bodies, experiences and things. We have that power to take one thing and turn it into something else, or to create from the void, from nothing, things as ideas, poetry, art, and so on.

How does God create? He gives an order. A clear directive statement is the first step of creation. God says: "There will be light!" Then he checks to see if his new creation is something he likes. If he likes it, he keeps it, if not he destroys it and starts over. This is the same process we all go through when creating any thing, even a meal. We start with "I desire food." We take an action: gather simple ingredients, mix them, apply heat and voila, we have a meal. It is almost as immediate as god's creations. When we create a new house or income level, or a relationship, it is a bit different from God's creation. We make the order and it takes time to arrive, or materializes. Here lies the difficulty that many experience. Once we make a demand, we need <u>faith</u> or <u>certainty</u> that what we just ordered is coming. When you go to a restaurant and order a burger, you know one is coming soon. When the waiter goes into the kitchen and is not back instantly with your burger, you don't go: "Oh, if burger is too hard to deliver. I'll have soup. No, I'll just have a toast and coffee. Oh forget it; I'm not hungry anymore." If you did that, you will go hungry. Yet this is exactly what we do with some of our creations, because we don't believe or trust that there is a burger with our name on it, or a house or a job and so on.

So, have you acknowledged yet that you are the creator of your world?

Are you willing to trust that your request will be fulfilled? Some times looking back in time and then into the present you may notice how all your wishes good and bad have come to be.

This too is in the Bible: Ask and you shall receive! What will you ask for if you have absolute knowing that the universe will deliver? Be careful, I asked for a partner whom I can't "twist around my finger", and I've been living with my creation for a long time now. I'm not complaining, just an awareness.

Say: I'm creator! And ask your body: Is it light or heavy?

6

CHOICE

Everything is a choice.

Where I'm today, that which I have or don't have and even who I am: all of those are the sum of my choices of yesterday. Even when it feels as if things just happened to me, such as winning the lotto, it is my choices, my actions and my willingness to experience those events that brings them into my life.

I worked with people age 18 to 70 that were mandated to attend Substance Abuse class by court order, because they had been caught driving under the influence of alcohol and other substances. They all felt they had no choice. They felt victimized by the system. They would tell stories of unfair police officers and judges, of hardship, of how good it feels to be high. What they could not see is how their choices created their experiences. They couldn't see that even in the present they had a choice to come to class or go to jail; to live or to die; to change or to continue on their self destructive course.

It is easy to see that the sofa I sit on in my living room is my choice, but most of us have difficult time seeing sudden illness, chronic disease, accidents, or storm as something we choose. People don't get up in the morning, stretch and say I'll have cancer or an accident today. What we do is we deny our needs. We push ourselves to a place where it appeasers as if, the only way to get what we need and long for, is to have a crisis. A crisis may give us permission to do what we wanted for a long time. A disaster makes it more socially acceptable to "act out". When we are sick or dying no one will judge us for leaving a job, leaving a relationship that no longer serves us, or taking time for ourselves. An emergency interrupts our pattern. We cannot continue to pretend that we are fine. The people in my class were tired of feeling sick, of fighting with friends and bosses, if they still had them. They were exhausted of pretending to be okay while having no money, no support and no energy left for anything, but chasing after the next fix. They needed something outside of them to pull them out of their private hell. When honest with themselves, they would tell me how worn out they are from hiding and keeping secrets and how difficult it is for them to change.

Crisis gives us opportunity for something else, for a change. And it is messy!

It is like when we were kids. We threw a tantrum when we did not get the candy or the attention we wanted. Eventually we got attention, even if it was a slap on the face. Disease is the slap on the face. We "ask" for change in the wrong way (tantrum), rather then attending to our needs in a way that will give us the candy (i.e., file for divorce, find a better job, move to a place we like and supports us, and so on). You can choose to interrupt your pattern without a crisis.

Realizing that I choose my life and everything in it, moment by moment, is a powerful thing. My experience today is the result of my choices in the past. The power in this knowledge is that:

What I created, I can un-create. I can change my life, or create something different all together. It is in my hands. Please note: Something different is not the same as change. An example for something different is a new dress. Altering a garment, say from a nightgown into a cocktail dress, is a change.

My past has nothing to do with my future. The past creates the present. Today, in the present, I can choose to experience that, which I created yesterday, or to change my thoughts, feelings, belief systems and my actions and create something else. When I do that my outcomes will change, believe it or not. It is the "You reap what you sow." So if I plant wheat, I'll reap wheat. In the present, though, I can exchange my wheat for corn, chickens, or something else. I do not have to eat wheat. That is my choice. I can also choose to plant something different, or to start a coop or a dairy farm. The choices are infinite. So the one time that we have power is this moment now. What we call the future is just a projection of our hopes and dreams. The future is a non-reality. The past is memory that we re-create in this moment, therefore also non-reality.

In each situation, we make the best choice with what we have at the time. No matter if we judge a situation as good or bad, there is benefit in it for us. We will talk about this later when discussing gratitude, but noticing the benefit in a situation is beneficial. For example: I had a tenant who all of a sudden stopped paying rent and was playing games with me. It irritated me even when I was not dealing with him. My mind was working overtime. I asked, what is the benefit in this, why am I creating that situation? When I asked that question, I no longer could be angry at, or focused on, my tenant. The answer is not logical and does not come from the head, but is more like knowing. In my story, it was. Oh, I asked to learn the legal system. My attorney has given me a booklet, which I did not read. And here I was, learning what it takes to evict a tenant the hard way. The benefit was my education.

When I see the benefit in an unpleasant experience, it always brings me to gratitude, not forgiveness. My tenant was playing a role in my private schooling, helping me learn the real estate laws. I'm grateful to him for his participation and what money I lost was fair pay for my education.

Sometimes we choose to never or always be like someone or not like someone. That is a limitation, not a true choice, because we do it on autopilot. For example, if I made a decision to not be like my mother, who was self-sacrificing, it is limiting and making me ineffective when some sacrifice may be required to get something I covet.

There are events around us that are a collective creation and they appear to be beyond our control. Still, it is us who choose to participate—or not—in them. I may throw a party, but you choose to come to it, or to stay home. Studies of airplanes crashes and train collisions show that some people make unconscious effort to miss those trips, while others go out of their way to be there.

What if everything in life is a choice, including whether to live or not? What if we make the best choice each time with what we have? What if it always has benefit for us? What if that which we have, who we are, and how we experience the world is the sum of our prior choices? What if the only thing that can create different outcomes is a choice in this moment, this present of time, now? What choice would you make if all things were possible? Who would you be? Where would you be? How would you be?

The past does not determine our future. The past is a memory we create in the present.

The future is not real; it is a projection of our desires and fears.

The present is where we create the past and the future. And we can change both now.

Ask: What else is possible here? What can I create that will be even better, even more fun?

7

ON THE FENCE

Indecision is wistful and ineffective. I can sit at a crossroad, debating which way is the best to take forever and ever. A better approach is to start walking. When I start walking, I'll soon notice signs that will let me know if I'm on the way to my target or not. I can then correct course if needed, but it will get me to my target sooner then insistence on making the right, best, or perfect choice.

When we look for the best or perfect choice, we start to second-guess ourselves. Having to be perfect has a chilling effect on creativity and action. We collect more and more information and the world passes us by. This is the story of the maiden who refused all the dignified young men that came to ask for her hand, and one day she found that she no longer has a line of suitors and ends up with an old and not-so-handsome partner, or ends up alone.

Don't be like the maiden! Get off the fence! Getting of the fence is making a decision and taking an action in that direction. <u>Imperfect action is better then perfect non-action.</u>

When we are undecided or on the fence, we feel as if we are on our own, unsupported. The contribution of the universe at such a time would be supporting us to sit on the fence and to keep the debate going. The universe and people can't contribute to us anything else. Telling us which way to take would be interference with our free will. As soon as we make a new choice, and start going that way, information, people, and resources will come our way to support us in this new request. Here is my story, to illustrate this point: I heard on a tape about a healer in South America, working with energy. My heart literally skipped a beat and I thought:

"Energy Healer! That is what I love to be! South America is too far!" A few months later, four people showed up in one day to tell me about Barbara Brennan School of Healing. I made decision to go to that school without knowing anything about it, besides that it teaches energy healing. That by itself this was quite amazing, to me, but wait for it, there is more. The school moved into "my backyard" and stayed there for the four years I attended. One day before I called the school, the faculty changed a rule that made it possible for me to attend right away. My father had given me money that made it easy to pay for the school. My story was not unusual at the Barbara Brennan School of Healing. When you start paying attention, you will discover the wonderful ways the universe twists itself to serve you. Isn't life magical?

So, sitting on the fence is a choice to not make a decision, and to not take an action.

We actually tell the universe we choose to sit there and it will support us in sitting there.

Make a choice and start moving in that direction and watch the universe rearranging to support you.

What else can you choose now?

8

TARGET

Having a target or making a choice or a demand about where you would like to be is the first step to getting there. Again, from the universe's point of view, if you wander without an aim, you choose to drift and the universe has to support you in that. Make a decision, take action, and keep going until you are there.

<u>It is not necessary to know how you reach your target</u>. Just have a target, put effort in that general direction and <u>never give up until you arrive.</u>

What is a target? It is a destination and the journey at once. Say you decide that you'd like to go to Florida for the warm climate. And say you have no idea where you are, but there is I-95, the road that goes across the U.S. You drive on it for some time and soon you notice that it is getting colder, and there are more pine trees and no palm trees. What do you do? Most likely, you turn around and start driving in the other direction. You do not say: "Bad road; I'm a stupid driver; everyone hates me; I'll never see Florida." But we do that with our talents and dreams. We say: "The economy is bad; I can't sing; no one likes my art; I'll never make it as a..." We give up and stop being the gift that we truly are.

<u>Celebrate your achievements!</u>

Be clear what is it you choose Florida for: the winds, the humidity, the beach, the palm trees, or something else? Sometimes we get exactly what we choose, but it is called the Bahamas or Hawaii, not Florida. Then all that is missing in our lives is noticing that we have arrived. Knowing that we have exactly what we ordered may look like a small thing, but it makes a big difference in the level of satisfaction and happiness we experience. There are many who are rich, but cannot see it and feel poor. Money is a struggle for them, even though they have lots of it. Realizing that you have reached your destination allows you to be nourished by your achievement and to set a new target. Keeping the old target will put you into a repetitive motion. That is you will keep accumulating money and feel poor.

So, do not forget to make a new target for yourself every so often.

Make your target achievable:

A target may look like this: "I choose to be a concert pianist and at least once, I'll play with an orchestra in a fabulous hall." It is a place to arrive at and it is a journey. It is attainable if you love to play the piano. Getting it depends on your efforts alone. Playing the piano is a reward in itself. Playing in an opera house is a consequence. It takes practice, practice, and practice. It takes consistency to create something.

People tell me how they pray every day for half an hour for abundance, for example. What they do not realize is that the rest of the time, 23 and half hours, they affirm, or pray, for exactly the opposite. They count the pennies, they say "I can't afford thi," they worry about the bills and so forth.

So, make your prayer an all-day practice.

Here, writing down your desires, creating a visual reminder you see throughout the day and playing as if you were there: by behaving, feeling and thinking as someone who is already rich and abundant, for example, is beneficial. It may be getting one thing of quality that makes you feel rich, or going to an open house as a potential buyer, experiencing what would it feel like to live there, or giving to someone less fortunate then you and making that person's day.

What would you create and be if money, education, and locality were not a consideration? Who would you be? How would your day look if it were your last day on earth?

In the Bible, it says that the world stands on study and awareness, work or action, good deeds toward others, or improvement of the collective wellbeing.

Some say: "I just want to hang out and watch TV." Well, that is a choice, too. There is no creative expression or action in it and it will not expand or contribute to the world. Those kinds of choices are the ones that create disease and pain. If that was my only purpose in life, then I could be a cow or a deer. I eat, I sleep, and I poop. At least as a cow or a deer, I provide milk and meat for others on the food chain (that is a contribution). To be clear, I have nothing against rest and watching TV. And if you choose that, I have no opinion about it, either. I like to bring to awareness to the different kind of target which that is.

A target that moves us forward and expands our world has to have all three elements: Choice, action, and contribution.

9

ATTENTION

That which we pay attention to, grows. What we do not pay attention to, escapes us. Magicians use this to their advantage. They create distraction to get us to pay attention in one place while they do something in another place, so we can't figure out what exactly they are doing. That's how they create the illusion of supernatural abilities.

We are all magicians. We are so good at distracting ourselves. We say we want a garden, but we never plant anything. We say we'd like to win the lotto, yet we never buy lotto tickets. We claim to be destined for greatness, and yet we sit watching TV. We look at actors, athletes, or the people on the news, thinking how lucky they are. What we choose not to see is that those people took a chance, worked hard, stumbled, and started over. They are uncertain, scared, and yet they put themselves out there, being true to themselves, defying parental and other good wishers' advice. We all are talented, capable, and amazing. The difference is that the winners of the world bet for their team. They invest in themselves. They trust their inner knowing of who and what they choose to be. They persist through failure to success. Many of us bet against ourselves, give up, and play it safe.

I heard this story from SCORE, an organization of retired executives who volunteer their time to help beginning entrepreneurs. UPS, a door-to-door delivery service, was first thought of as a paper for an MBA class. The paper got a "B" and the comment that it is unpractical. Who would pay for door-to-door delivery when there is perfectly good postal service? Most of us would have stopped right there. The young founders of UPS were focused on their target, not paying attention to the small-minded teacher's remarks. The day they opened their doors, they had one client. Some would see this as a failure, a sign to give up. The UPS CEO saw it as a success.

<u>Attention is necessary for learning, for growth, for getting what we like. Pay attention! Pay attention to that which you like to have more of. Put your attention on YOU. What makes you happy, what feels good to you, what you like and desire; where and what you choose to be. Keep your attention on your target!</u>

Pay attention to you!

I'm my own business; my health, my happiness, my career or my money, my success – that is my business and my responsibility. That is where my attention is.

My children, partner, parents, and so forth are not my business. It is impossible to make another person happy, or anything else. When we put on a partner the demand to be happy, strong, or to be an "A" student, we are placing a big burden on their shoulders. It is a waste of my energy and obstacle to them. They have the right to choose who and what they like to be, just as I do.

<u>Track the big picture! Do not get distracted by the small details!</u>

Someone pointed out that McDonald's is in the business of real estate, not hamburgers. At first, it sounded weird. But then, consider the burgers McDonald's delivers. I have hard time calling anything that McDonald's serves "food". Now, consider the locations of McDonald's establishments. For me, it was an eye-opener. They are on every prime commercial corner in the world. When they opened a large store next to the famed coffee houses of Vienna, Austria, they did not advertise burgers. They called themselves a coffee house and advertised paper cups.

<u>The moral of this story is that it is crucial to know what it is we are after and put our attention and efforts there.</u>

Many clients are so good at telling me what their partner wants, or what they don't want. Knowing what you don't want is a good start. Then move to how would your life be without the thing you don't like and make that your target. Focus on the things you like to have more of.

What do you like your life to look like in a year? In 5 years? Don't say, "I'd like to be debt-free." Instead say, "I have more money than I can spend."

Pay attention to what you like to create!

Put your thoughts on paper. Then you can examine your thoughts one at the time, so they are not tangled and confusing. The writing process forces you to have more clarity. Putting your feelings on paper eventually creates space in you, and it helps you to focus on you. Keeping a journal can ease your decision-making, reduce stress, give you insight, and open your mind to new possibilities. A journal also is a great way to track your progress. It is yours and need not be politically correct or literal. Writing in your journal can be one way you pay attention to yourself.

10

TRUST

<u>Trust is the antidote to worry</u>. I may not be able to avoid the thought of worry, but I do not have to believe it. I can choose to replace an intrusive thought with a thought that supports me. For example: if I do not hear from my kids, I believe it is because they are having such a good time that stopping to call home doesn't enter their minds. I trust that when they want my input, they know how to find me. I trust them to take care of themselves. <u>Trust in someone else comes from trust in me.</u>

<u>This is how self-esteem is built. Self-esteem is trust in me.</u> When I started to do the things I said I'll do, my trust in me grew. I'm talking about the small stuff such as dishes and laundry and finishing school and so on. Each accomplishment made the next step more attainable.

Writing this book may not be a big deal for some, but for me, it is a huge step of trust. I'm an immigrant. I left the continent and the country and language I knew twice in my adult life. English is my third language. That by itself is a big disadvantage. I'm also dyslexic and frankly "can't spell to save my life" in any language. Computers, of course, are a big help. What gives me the trust and courage to even venture into writing a book is the fact that I finished my Master's Degree in Social Work, writing many big papers in English and some of them even got A's. So if I could do that, I can do this. My belief that I can do anything I choose to do, and my attention to the inner push of my soul to do something to create ease and peace and joy in this world, are what make this book possible.

People talk of luck: the luck of an understudy actress who gets her big brake when the leading role actress breaks her leg or gets the flue; the luck of a chance meeting with the person who invests in your painting or

30

business. When we look at luck more closely it presents the following formula: preparation + courage + opportunity = luck.

This is how we work: When an opportunity presents itself, our mind does a calculation of all the accomplishments and all the unfinished tasks. When the scale is right we go for it, we trust in ourselves and have the courage to make a leap into the unknown, the lead role, the big business, and so on. When the list of things we promised and did not deliver is way longer then our accomplishments, we don't trust in our capacity to fill the new shoes and it feels as too big an effort for just another disappointment, and sometimes we don't even see the opportunity. What is interesting here is that dirty dishes and unfinished books have the same weight. It is just that: if you say you choose to do something, do it, if you choose not to do something, do not do it. Trust is not something you have. <u>Trust is a consistency of action</u>. You may be consistent for 100 years; it matters little if you are not today. This is easy to see in sports. A team will choose you based on your prior performance, and fire you, often, after one failure to deliver.

When I trust myself, I can trust others. People often think that to trust means to hope that others will do what we like them to do. That is not so. I trust you to be you. If you are always late, I trust you to be late. If you always do what you say you'll do, I trust you will deliver.

<u>To trust therefore requires one to know oneself and the other.</u>
<u>Trust is the antidote to jealousy, doubt, fear, regret, and worry.</u>
Can you trust you to show up for yourself?

One way to show up for yourself is to simply replace all your unsupportive thoughts and feelings, with the statement: "I TRUST" or "I'M TRUST". It is as if you choose to not watch violence on TV. You see that there is crime-solving episode and you switch to the music or comedy channel. Over time, the broken record in your head is no longer there. You truly are trusting in your own capacity. Then others will see you as trustworthy, too.

Do it with the same commitment you take a pill your doctor prescribed. Do it with the same urgency as an addict searching for their next fix. The beauty of this medicine is that it costs you nothing and it has many positive side effects and not a single negative one.

<u>Some of the positive side effects are fearlessness and freedom to be you.</u>
Don't take my word for it, please! Do it for you and prove it to yourself.

11

CONTROL

Control is choosing our emotions to give us a desirable outcome.

Control is one of the most commonly misunderstood concepts.

The English, among others, believe that control is to have a poker face. It doesn't matter how you feel as long as your "friends" and society at large think you are composed, and you behave with polite mannerisms that someone, somewhere, decided is acceptable. They actually teach you to be incongruent with yourself. That is not the control I'm talking about.

Then there is the control we attempt to put on others and the environment. People who have lost control over their emotions, thoughts, and actions try to control the environment. Abusers, as an example, often say to their partner, "If you didn't do this, then I wouldn't hit you." The problem is that the partner and his/her behavior is not the source of the anger and violence in the abuser and therefore compliant behavior of the partner cannot stop the abuse, ever. There is a way to stop it, though.

In the Tarot cards, there is the Strength card. In one of the Tarot decks, it depicts a female figure facing a lion. She has nothing but her bare hands, and yet the lion is tamed. It is the person's inner strength that causes a fierce animal to submit willingly. It is respect for each other's nature and love that binds them. The lion represents emotions and the wild nature in us. What will it take for you to have that control over the lion in you?

The control I'm talking about is more like in the Strength card: it is control over your feelings, emotions, thoughts and actions. It is not about suppressing your feelings. It is about choosing the feelings and emotions and thoughts and actions that support you and are harmonious with the environment, at once. I give my clients this example: you go to a club and the comedian looks at you and says, "You idiot!" Everyone laughs, and so do you. When you leave the club, someone bumps into you. They turn and say, "You idiot, watch where you're going!" You are slightly irritated, but move on and life is good. Then you arrive home and your significant other says, "Where on earth have you been, you idiot?" What is your reaction? Be honest.

What is the difference in those three scenarios? Why do you respond differently to the same statement? Is it because of the meaning you give each one of them? If you gave the same meaning to all three, would you feel and react the same? And who chooses the meaning? You do!

The first one was the punch line of a joke – funny.

The next one is just some jerk who you will never meet again – no big deal.

The third is personal- it is significant and intended to hurt you.

Is it really intended to hurt you? When you say things, is it to hurt others or to defend yourself? And is there really anything to defend, except the concept of ego, which is not real by definition. How would it look if instead of defending yourself from the perceived attack, you put a white flag out and ask something like, "Wow, you must have had a really bad day. What's going on?" How would this scene play out and end? The same way or different?

Control is choosing our emotions to give us a desirable outcome.

If your outcome is not what you like, you are out of control. It is an inner job. When you put your attention outside of you, you are out of control. You give your power to people, situations, and things. When you take responsibility for your feelings, thoughts, emotions, and deeds, you take your power back.

One of the deadliest and most anger creating things you can do is to give your power away. When I say, "You make me angry!" I give my power to you. You have the key to my peacefulness and to my anger. When I say, "I'm angry." I take responsibility for my feelings. Now I can ask, what is this about? What do I want and what am I unwilling to give to myself? Once you get the awareness of what need is denied, you have the power to give it to your self. I used to get very angry at some artwork hanging on museum walls. Following this process, I realized that what I needed is to be an artist, to paint. I was blocking my creative impulse. Once I started to create my own art, the museum did not evoke anger in me any more.

We give our power away with the words that we use.

We negate our potency when we give in to avoid conflict or to preserve a relationship when we play it safe or small.

We are not true to ourselves when we make things, situations, and people bigger than ourselves, or significant.

Significance is when we make something so very important. For example: I have 100-year old vase, passed down through the generations in my family. It is very important to me to keep it safe and pass it to the next generation, to my kids. One day my 5-year old, out of curiosity, takes the vase, trips, and breaks it. At that moment, it is like something in me is broken, the anger in me rises, and I scream at my child, for whose sake I guarded the dumb thing anyway. Ironic, isn't it? If, on the other hand, I can see the vase as just a vase, I may be more concerned with my child and attend to her safety, in a caring way.

What have you made bigger then you? Note: it can be a person, a situation, a feeling, a thought, anything.

Do you feel light or heavy when you give your power away?

12

MOTIVATION

Have you ever felt lazy? Did you ever find yourself unable to get out of bed or turn off the TV and do the list of things you put in front of yourself? You know you should do those things, but your whole being is resisting?

Have you ever called yourself dumb, or stupid, or judged your self as ugly, not good, or not enough?

I have. I remember a day in my twenties: I felt low and down, my space was a mess, my hair was a disaster, I just wanted to be left alone to hide… and then someone I liked called and said that he was in the area and would I like to get together in 30 minutes? I said, "Sure, come, I'm home." Somehow my place, that for weeks was an oppressive mess, was clean and presentable in moments; I was in and out of the shower, dressed and pretty, all in less then half an hour. Was I lazy or did I need an ounce of motivation? I needed motivation.

It was years later that I realized that there are no lazy people! There are only motivated and not motivated people!

Addiction is a case of motivation. Have you ever seen a drug user's motivation to get his or hers next fix? We develop a relationship with a game, substance, work, sport, or whatever. It gives us something we want: relaxes us, distracts us, and makes us more social or easier to be alone. And it has demands on us, mainly to maintain the relationship. When we see the benefit of our chosen addiction as bigger then the cost of maintaining it, we have a difficult time giving it up. When the cost becomes higher then the benefits, real or perceived, we can start on the road of recovery. Now there is motivation for change.

So what motivates you? And what is killing your motivation? I find that,

that which you choose is fun and easy to do, while that which you must do, have to be or do, or should do, is a motivation killer.

Check it for yourself.

Say: I have to do X – does it feel light or heavy?

Now say: I choose to do X – does it feel light or heavy?

In part two, we will look at the way words like should and have to influence the way we feel and act.

PART II

13

HERE COME THE DIRTY WORDS!

In this section, we will look at the small ways in which we sabotage ourselves, the ways we get in our own way. Those are the things we do and say that keep as ineffective, small, and stuck. We will discuss words, opinions, and beliefs that we have learned from others or from our own experience, those words that do not support us and render us less productive and feeling like life is a struggle.

An explanation is needed here. Everything is energy. Einstein proved that mass is energy mathematically. We are energy and our consciousness is swimming in a sea of energy. We vibrate at a range of frequencies and we are capable and do pick up thoughts, emotions, feelings, ideas and pain from our environment and others in our range of frequencies. The person or situation may be near or far, true or false, past or present, dead or alive. One way to detect whether it is our own energy or not is by noticing sudden change in mood or self-talk that is non productive or even mean. Ask yourself, "Is it mine?" Sometimes the energy we pick-up on is so close to our own vibration and so familiar that we tend to buy into it as ours, instantly. For example, if you feel a headache. You can ask, "Is it mine?" and see if it goes away. Most of us just say, "Oh, I have a headache," and with that we make it ours.

What is interesting here is that we mean well when we take the pain of others. We may be attempting to heal them. The problem is that the other person is a creator, too. When they have not asked you to facilitate them in healing their headache, they'll just create more pain. Remember, there is benefit to that person in having a headache. So we waste our energy and theirs as well.

Resistance works in similar way. Think of it as pulling or pushing onto a person. When they resist, it makes you pull/push even harder. From an energetic point of view, you are an equally formidable power and that creates a stuck place for both of you. Allowance, which requires no judgment, is what can resolve the standstill, and then it turns into a dance. We create resistance with our judgments. For example: I demand that my son clean his room. That is a push. I judge his room to be dirty. It may also be an observation, but I demand he do something on my schedule. If he is unwilling to clean his room, he is resisting. He judges me as interfering in his business. If we choose to maintain our positions, of me demanding and him saying no, we will find ourselves in a stuck place, and in an ongoing argument. I can choose to let him have his room any way he likes, or I can clean it myself. He can choose to clean his room when asked or on his own initiative. Either of those would be allowance. Then we have nothing to argue about. We can go out and play.

When you feel stuck, ask yourself:

- What is it?

- Is it mine?

- What awareness is here for me?

- Is there anything I need to do or be different?

- Does it support me to feel, think, or be this way?

- If I love myself, would I think, feel, or behave this way toward me?

- What other possibilities are here?

14

MOTIVATION KILLERS

Constantly looking outside of you, attempting to guess the wishes and desires of another in order to make them happy so you can be happy, or putting yourself on hold until you achieve this or have that, are behaviors that kill motivation. This never works. At the beginning, it appears to be a motivator, but it lets us down, even when we are successful at what we were chasing. A bit like addiction, isn't it?

Do you say to yourself - I have to do this, or I must go there, or I ought to know this by now? Right now, think of something you have to do, or you should do. Now notice how it feels in your body. Is there heaviness; a resistance? For, example say, I have to do the laundry. Is it true? Do you feel like the boss, big, light, or peaceful, or do you feel tight, small, or heavy? Now say, I choose to do the laundry today so I have nice-smelling clothes. Or you can say, I choose not to do the laundry today. Today, I'll watch all the episodes of this show. Notice how it feels in your body. Is it lighter? Do you feel bigger or smaller? What is your truth? Play with this. The distinction gets easier with practice.

Words that kill your motivation: Disempowering words.

Should/shouldn't, must/must not, can't, have to, may not.

Replace them with I choose to/I choose not to.

Now imagine I stand in front of you and insist that you do the dishes. They are my dirty dishes and I say that you have to wash them. What is your reaction? Can I really make you do them? Of course, if I offer to give you $200 to wash my dishes (raising the benefit), you may choose to wash them, but if you think it's my problem, my turn – would you do them? Can I make you do anything you do not want to do?

My answer to this question is NO. I'll do or be what I choose to do and be. We make our choices by what <u>appears</u> to have higher value for us in the moment. When I say, "I choose" or "I choose not to..." I avow to this truth.

Notice that, if you are not doing something, you are choosing not to do it. Acknowledge that and see if it feels lighter, more empowering of you. What do I mean by this? I'm from Israel. Many Israelis living in the U.S. say: "I wish I could go back." The energy of that statement is that of a victim. The truth is that Israel would welcome them with open arms. The only thing preventing them from going back to Israel is their choice. They have chosen and continue to choose to live in the U.S.

The word "can't" is in a league of its own. When you say you can't do, be, or have something, you make that thing bigger then you. You give your power to that thing. And then you work hard to demonstrate that you can't. You may have heard this: if you think you can – you can; if you think you can't – you can't. So which would you choose? Which choice puts you on your team?

15

BUT AND TRY

Get off your "but"!

Have you ever said I like to go, but... Do you know someone who says things like, "I'd like to come to your party, but..."? or, "I'd like to go back to work, but..." or, "I'd like this, but I can't afford it," and so on.

How do you feel? Does it irritate you, or do you feel closer to that person? Does the other person feel in charge of their life, or do they feel like a victim?

What am I really saying when I use the word "but"? I'm saying, I have a different priority. I'm saying, "Sorry, I have homework, I will not make it." Now notice how this statement feels. Does it ring truer and more affirming of you as the receiver? Now check it as if you are using it. That feels lighter, too, doesn't it?

Anything after the BUT is a justification, excuse, negates the first part, and creates a lie with truth attached to it. This is one of the stickiest things. The truth is we choose to or choose not to do, have, be, or go. Every time we use the word "but", or feel a need to explain anything, we are lying to ourselves as well as to others, creating confusion in our lives and in the lives of those people closest to us. That confusion keeps us small and powerless.

So, are you willing to know the truth, to let go of explanations, reasoning, and justifications? Would you choose to say no to "BUT" or "because" from now on, at least for 30 days?

Stop trying!

"Trying" is another way we keep ourselves stuck.

There is no action in trying. If you get up off your chair, you got off your chair; if you didn't, you chose not to. When you say, "I'm trying to get up," you are lying to yourself as if the action is bigger then you. What have you made bigger then you? And if you made it so, can you change it now? "Trying" states, "I'd like to, but I can't so far." This is a combination of two forbidden words at once. Either do it, or admit you choose not to do it. The truth will empower you to move to something else that is more in line with you. Trying is wasteful of your time and a lie about your ability. Stop trying and make a choice!

You may say:
- I'm working on...
- My intention is to...
- I'm in the process of...

Notice that those statements have action in them.
Have fun playing with empowering language!

16

WANT AND NEED

"I want" means I lack; that I do not have.

What if having the thought of something is an indication that this something is already yours in some realm, and the only thing keeping it away from you in this reality is your affirmation of "I want."

"I'm willing to have a big house" will get you in one much faster than saying "I want a big house."

I like …

I choose…

I prefer…

Need, similarly, indicates not having. We use the word need to indicate desire. Differentiate between need, desire, or want. Needs are basic survival requirements. From an energy point of view we need nothing. Using the word "need" leads to greed. There is a saying: "You can't have enough of what you don't really want." Think of an alcoholic – they can never have enough alcohol. That is because they truly are seeking something else: inner peace, courage, acceptance, or forgiveness – not alcohol.

Here again "I choose" is so much more potent and productive. Choice leads to awareness.

So use I choose, or I choose not.

17

FINISHING THE SENTENCE

Have you ever scared yourself to death by saying, "I don't know what I'll do if... he /she leaves, if I lose this job..." fill in the blank. It is a known fact that most people will choose what they know rather then venture into the unknown, even if the known stinks and the unknown has promise for a much better outcome. An unfinished sentence creates an unknown.

This is a true story: I would say to my toddler son, "I'll count to three and you better be in bed," and surprisingly, he would go to bed. Later he would count by himself: one, two, two and a quarter, and just before, three he'd do the task. This is the power of the unfinished sentence. By not finishing your sentence, you are stressing yourself and you compel yourself to do what may not be in your best interest.

So here is another possibility: Choose to finish your sentence and ask: What is the worst outcome if this happened: loss of job, loss of relationship, I die...? Usually when we look at the worst-case scenario, it feels lighter then the unfinished sentence and the least desirable outcome is way more manageable then the unknown. In addition, if you look at the possibility of the worst-case scenario happening, it is often unlikely to happen, statistically speaking. Again, not finishing your sentences has the power of blackmailing. The blackmail has no power over you if you choose to accept the threat and deal with the consequences, rather then avoiding them. That is, if my spouse learns about my indiscretions, he may divorce me. He may also chose not to divorce me. If the relationship is worthwhile, it may survive an incident. The truth is always better then a net of cover-ups. Indiscretion and lies are always worse than just indiscretion.

The truth has a way of reviling itself. My personal preference is to finish the sentence and have no secrets from others or myself.

So let's look at another example: what is the worst that can happen if you lose your job? Well, you may have to sell your home or move to a cheaper rental, or even move to a relative for some time. It is unpleasant. The chances are, sooner or later you will find yourself in a new environment, with new opportunities that are oftentimes more suited to your being. For example, you move to a small village and your hobby becomes your vocation, and you are now getting paid to play. In other words, you end up having a life that is a lot more fun!

Remember, you are the creator of your world, and everything you create has some benefit for you.

18

WORRY

What is worry? <u>Worry is us using our imagination against ourselves.</u> It is imagining the worst outcome, the one we least desire, and projecting it into the future. When we worry, we do not have trust. Jealousy, doubt, regrets, and fear are all worries!

<u>Worry is creative</u>: we use our imagination and emotions and we put a lot of attention on the subject of our worry. That is a creative process. The problem is that we create that which we do not choose to experience and when it shows up we feel as a victim. Worry is a wasteful use of our energy. We can act only in the present moment. When we worry, we live in the future. We are distressed by an event that has not transpired yet, an event that is not real. So there is no action that we can take; that is: our kids are not yet in trouble, our lover has not yet cheated on us, or the milk hasn't spilled yet. In a way, it is a bit like trying, but while trying is no-action, worry is active. We are actively using our minds to create a reality we do not like to experience. When we worry, we feel the irritation and the fear, and our body reacts as if the event has transpired. Our body is reacting over and over again to a stressor that is made up. It is like watching horror movies all the time—it makes us sick.

The opposite is true, too. If you watch lighthearted movies that make you laugh, over time you will feel better! If you visualize the kids being well, your partner being faithful and so on, the chances are they will be so.

Here is a short version of the secret of creating. It truly is not a secret. We all know and use the so-called "secret" all the time. The trouble is, we do it unintentionally. To create on purpose: <u>Focus on that which you choose to create, put emotion, thought, and feel energy into it as if it were</u>

48

there already, take an action toward it and trust it will be delivered. Simple, isn't it?

When we worry we are in the future. One way to stop worrying is to bring yourself into the present. What is true in this moment now? What do I really know? I know that my kids have not called me in the last two days. That's it. Worrying about them is giving that information unwanted interpretation, one that does not please me. In this present moment, I have the power to not interpret the two days without communication as a sign of problem, or to take it to mean something that pleases me, like, "They are well and having fun, and they have no time for phone calls."

A good reason not to worry habitually is that it numbs our awareness. When we worry or live in fear all the time, we can't tell when there is real danger to us or to someone dear to us. It is like the story of the boy who cried wolf. We can't tell real awareness that something is wrong from a false projection.

Worry puts us at the mercy of our thoughts and feelings. It is making our feelings the boss of us. Is that true or false? Say, "I'm bigger than my thoughts and feelings" and check if it feels light or heavy.

Use repetitively "I TRUST" as mantra and antidote to worry.

What you trust in is your ability to deal with whatever presents itself when it is here.

19

LOVE

Love is an overused, confusing word. What does it really mean?

Most people practice conditional love. It is a bargaining system. You do this for me and I'll do that for you. As with everything else, this system has value. It is more efficient. I'm better at bringing money to the unit; you are better at keeping the house and children functioning. And as everything else, it has a shadow side when we attach our love for each other to the things we bargained for, and when we forget that we are the source of all things for ourselves. In conditional love, there is the statement of, "I'll not give those thing to myself; you have to give them to me." This makes our partner the source of our good. We create a false "GOD". There is a hidden belief that the only way to be happy or safe is to get something from a partner as if we do not have that in ourselves.

Indications of conditional love are phrases like, "I love you, but you have to do this for me!" or "You are such a good boy/girl, I love you so much!" Those statements are subtle, but if we take the time to consider the actual meaning behind our words and actions, we'll find the conditions we set up for our love. Most of us confuse passion and fear of being alone with romantic love. What we call chemistry is just that; chemistry. We have a new endorphins-inducing experience in the presence of a person. We ironically associate or assign the good feelings that the endorphins create in us to the partner. We believe that we need that person in order to have the good feeling.

And then we have power over others. Power over is not love at all. It is attempt to control the other, or the environment, to give us that which we decided we would not give to ourselves. In the extreme, we may believe our existence depends on making sure the other give us what we "need". When we focus on the other or the environment we are not in touch with ourselves. We have divorced ourselves in order to stay in a relationship and hoped that the other will deliver. The problem is that no one can give us that which we are unwilling to give to ourselves.

This tendency to put down one's partner is often an indication of pending divorce. Couples that can stay on subject when arguing have mach better prognosis for long-lasting relationship.

Love is a state-of-being, not a feeling.

Unconditional Love is a state of being. Unconditional Love is generalized kindness and caring toward all beings, including one's self. It has no sacrifice in it.

Mother Theresa and the Dalai Lama embody unconditional love. Some mothers are capable of it, too. Unconditional love is acceptance of what is, acceptance of the other without judgment, and acceptance of oneself. There are no victims, no winners, and no losers. Seeing everything as one is the quality of unconditional love.

What I give you – I give to myself; what I deny you – I deny myself.

So how do we get out of conditional love and move toward unconditional love?

1. Make a decision to love. It is best to start with you. Most may find that hard. So you may choose to love your partner. I love my spouse because he/she is the parent of my children, for example. That will never change and has no demand in it. This kind of love has appreciation in it, gratitude for one's self and the other. Take care of something: a plant, an animal, or a human being.

2. Practice Acceptance. We are not in unconditional love if we are in judgment. A quality of unconditional love is acceptance of what is. Acceptance is not agreeing, it is more like a detached observer noticing what is, without giving it (the situation, the behavior, the words) an interpretation or meaning. For example: I was dishonest with you. You probably know I have a tendency to twist the truth. But this time, it is you that I mislead. Can you still love me? I was being me. You might not like it, and you may choose not to play with me any longer, but can you still love me? It is a bit like when a child grows up, leaves the parent's home, and chooses a path or a partner not exactly to the parents' taste. Do we disown her, or do we love her just the same?

3. Practice letting go. Choose to release your loved one from all the things you want from him/her. Simply use the mantra "I release you." When you do it mindfully, the unspoken demands and conditions you put on your partner will pop up. You can the release them one by one. You may notice that the things you demand from your partner are needs you have and that you are unwilling to give them to yourself. We say: you will

provide for me, you have to respect me, or you have to be faithful to me. We assign the other our financial wellbeing, our respectability, or our sense of trustworthiness. All the while, we refuse to be and give those things to ourselves. We make the other the source and in that we give our power away. By choosing to take back the demand from your partner and to provide for your own needs, you empower yourself. You also create energetic space between you, which becomes an invitation for him/her to step in closer to you, or to move away. The point is that this ultimately frees you and empowers you. Instead of asking to be fed a fish, you now are learning how to fish for yourself.

You are the source of your world, your money, and your honor. You are love. The partner is merely the channel through which you created those things. In what other way can you receive those things?

I saw a slogan on a desk in Oregon that asked: "What would love do?" I love it. If we act with this question as guiding principle, humanity will be way more humane.

Who and what will you be if you love you?

Love has quality of the more you give, the more you get.

What if you put your attention on giving love?

Just like a breath: when you exhale, inhaling is automatic. When you give love, love comes to you threefold.

PART III

20

YOU ARE THE SOURCE

What if you are never wrong?

What if you are the only one who knows what's best for you? What if every choice you make has a purpose and a benefit for you? What if there are no mistakes, only learning experiences?

What if watching TV will give you the idea that will change the world? What if not going to work today will save your life? What if having a car accident will bring you to the love of your life, or to your purpose?

What if you can go through life being you, choosing for you, doing what you love, and having gratitude for whatever shows up? How would your life look then? Would you be motivated to get up in the morning?

How would you be without judgment, guilt, regret, or expectations? Know that at any given time, you are choosing the best option for you. That whatever the outcome, it has benefit for you and it is just a game of creation. If you like your creation - you keep it. If you do not - start over. Create something else. Life is an adventure, an exploration, and an expedition to discover you. Discover your beauty, wisdom, joy, sorrow, pain, and healing capacity.

Now there is one thing that is entirely up to you and will make all the difference in the world. And that is ACTION. Not perfect action, just action. What would you do if you couldn't go wrong? What if you are the highest authority on you?

You can read many books on love, but you do not know love until you experience it. Experience is the one true teacher.

My son was a stubborn little toddler. We covered all the electric outlets and he, as small as he was, learned to pull the covers out. One day he put a hairpin in the outlet, got shocked, and never again did I have to cover the outlets. He then knew that it is not fun to stick pins in those things. He learned pain.

So, the point here is that every experience has a benefit and that regret is a worthless way to spend your energy. Asking, "What is the benefit in this situation?" will effortlessly bring you to gratitude.

21

WHAT CAN WE LEARN FROM A FLY?

Have you ever watched a fly caught in your house? The fly will go to the light. The thing is, an open window usually is darker then a closed one. So when it refuses to go to the dark open window, it dies. But if it takes a chance and flies into the dark, it is home free, literally.

So what does it mean? If you go this way and you feel like you are hitting your head on the wall, stop, take a breath and do something different. It may not make logical sense; it may feel as if you are going backward or giving up. That's OK. Keep your target in front of you, and do something different.

I often share this story with my clients: You are driving from point A to point B. In the middle of the road, there is an obstacle; say a boulder is blocking the road. If you insist on going the way that is blocked, you may have to wait for a few hours or days. Or, you may take the detour and get to where you're going on time.

The principle here is one of effortless being. Friends of mine were looking for their first home. They made an offer on a house, but nothing was going right. One day, they drove in a neighborhood just beyond their price range. They saw a "for sale" sign and asked to see the house. The sellers had moved to a new home and had to sell quickly. The deal went quickly and effortlessly. My friends got the house for a great price. When they moved into the home, their furniture fit perfectly and it felt as if they have been there forever. This house was bigger, in a better neighborhood, and cheaper than the one that had looked at before where the deal had fallen apart.

22

WE PLAN, GOD LAUGHS!

Do you know the story of the Post-it, the little squares of colorful paper that stick and un-stick? The inventors of that stick and un-stick glue were looking to create permanent glue that cannot be undone. Someone spilled some of the ingredients on the floor and the stick/un-stick glue was born. This is God's finger in our stew. If we take it and say: "Wow, what can I do with this?" - We change the world! If we insist on permanent glue, we miss the opportunity to bring the post-it into the world.

You pray for more money. You say, "Dear God, I need additional $300 per month. Please, GOD!" And what happens? You get fired from your job. You panic and ask for your job back. So you get it back, or another one like it. What if instead you said, "OK! Where is my job with the $300 or more in salary? You relax in the certainty that there is something better for you. Soon, you get a new job with better pay, better boss, and nicer coworkers.

You had to lose the job that pays X in order to get the job that pays X+$300, and it takes a moment for the universe to rearrange it self to give you that.

I asked for a bench, and for some time, I looked at purchasing one. I couldn't find any I liked and the price always seemed too high. Then one day, a woman who had sold her house was in the process of moving out and putting furniture on the side of the road. She was getting rid of a bench just like the one I wanted. I asked if it was OK to take it, and she helped put it in my car for free. Would you stop to ask for your bench, or drive on, insisting on a new one? Do you welcome God's intervention in your business, or are you Like Joseph? Joseph who?

Joseph was a God-fearing man. He trusted God and praised him all day long. One day, a flood came to Joseph's hometown. Everyone evacuated, but Joseph said, "I trust in God, he'll save me." A rescue car came, but Joseph wouldn't go. Later, when the water was up to 4 feet high, a boat came to take Joseph to safety, but he would not go. "God will save me," he said. Then a helicopter came to lift Joseph from the roof of his house, but Joseph insisted that God would be his savior. Eventually, Joseph stood before God and he asked, "Dear God, what happened? I trusted you! Why did you forsake me?" And God responded, "Dear Joseph, I do not know. I wondered what happened myself? I send you a car, and a boat, and a helicopter. What are you doing here?"

Joseph was looking for some miracle, and judged the "human intervention" as not good enough for him. As if the rescue efforts were outside of "God's plan".

So: Do not judge, insisting to get you request this way or that way. Accept it if it fits your target, even when it is not exactly a match to your imagination.

Celebrate who you are, your creativity. The way something comes to you is less important than the fact that it comes to you.

Give thanks for what you have and then ask for even better! When you are grateful for the bench from the side of the road, you get even more benches.

Beyond all, take an ACTION!

If I did not stop and ask for the bench, I wouldn't have it. If Joseph had evacuated and left with the car or the boat, he would be safe. If my friends had insisted on the first house or gave up, they would not have their dream home.

23

THE RIPPLE EFFECT

Sometimes we see the full affect our actions have on others, or we see some of it; sometimes we do not. Sometimes we judge our creations as good or bad, but from a wider point of view and/or the perspective of time, we may see the bad as good and vice-versa. It is like the pay-it-forward idea. You choose to give to someone, just for the fun of it, and they do something new and different and that creates difference in the world. It may not be what you expected, but being different and new makes the playground more fun, doesn't it?

In the movie Hugo, there is this boy who is an orphan, living alone in the clock building of a train station, taking care of the clock and working on restoring this mechanical toy. All he needs to make it work is a small, simple screw. Later in the movie, he befriends a girl and one night, as they are in the clock tower looking at the stars, he tells her that machines and toys all come with the exact parts needed, no extra parts. And he has figured out that since this universe is like a machine, there must be a reason why he is in the world, because there are no unimportant parts, even if you are a simple screw.

I like that story, don't you? We may not all be equal per se, but we all are needed for this universe to work. Like our bodies: All cells start exactly the same. Then each gets a specialty. One is a blood cell, another is a liver or a skin cell, and so on. Each cell has a job to do. When all the cells do their job faithfully, the body is well and we are happy.

Fundamentally, people are all the same - energy and consciousness in play. We are creations that procreate and create. We are all important and perfect, just the way we are.

So, know that you matter, you are important, and you are exactly in the right place.

There are no mistakes.

24

I'M GOD

"I'm" is a powerful word. What you put after it is created. I'm power, I'm a creator, I'm an artist, I'm a lover, I'm joy, I'm money, I'm smart, I'm talented, I'm music, I'm strong, I'm beautiful, I'm control, I'm choice. Say this and see how it feels in your body: light or heavy? Is it true or isn't it? And what if you fill your head with this self-talk: I'm power, I'm joy, I'm… In the Bible, God repeats "I'm God" all the time. If it works for him, it works for me, too. How about you?

"You are" is creative to. It is creative when we buy the opinions of others about who we are. Some times it is helpful to us, and sometimes it is not. I say, if it supports you, then buy it; if it doesn't, you have a choice not to believe it and then it does not affect you.

25

BELIEFS

Your explicit and unspoken beliefs create and color your reality. If you believe that something is bad, it will be bad for you and if you believe that it's good, it will be good for you. You can also choose to not see things on the spectrum of good and bad. For example: some believe that cold weather makes them stronger, some believe that if they are exposed to cold they'll get sick, and some just register it as a neutral observation—oh, it's cold today. It is this last neutral way of seeing events that creates freedom of choice.

If you are superstitious, I find it helpful to make the superstition work for you. For example: I believe that if a black cat is crossing my way, it is a good omen; that the number 13 is a lucky number; that an itch in my palm will bring money to me, and that if I ask Josephine, the parking angel, for a parking spot, she will always find me one. This usually works for me and creates a fun anticipation to see how my luck will play out.

What do you believe in? Does it work for you or against you and is it your idea, or did you buy it from someone else? In this moment, you can choose differently. You can choose what supports you, what feels good, and what is honoring of you.

Sometimes we make these determent conclusions, decisions, and promises. We swear to ourselves that we will never be something or that we will always be something. This creates limiting beliefs, and prevents us from having full spectrum choice in the moment. Are you willing to take back and erase all the promises, decisions, vows, and commitments? When you do, you have the freedom to choose what works for you in the present.

How do we take back beliefs that are hidden? We recognize their effects by looking at where we are stuck. When something doesn't work in our lives, it is an indication that two opposing forces or belief systems are at play. For example: I want a job. I've sent my resume to many employers and gone to interviews and I still do not have a job. I ask myself, what is the benefit in not having a job? It may be that I think I'll miss the sunlight working all day, or lose my freedom to travel, or that I'm not good enough and will be found out. It is not logical. I look at whether those beliefs are supportive of my desire to have a job. Then, I consciously create beliefs that are supportive of having employment. For example: Having a job is freedom to travel more. I have a unique contribution and my employer appreciates it, I take a walk on my lunch break and enjoy the sunlight.

Doing this process in writing is way more effective and recording your new believes is necessary. Old beliefs have habit to come back unless we firmly replace them. It is like cleaning a pile of shirts and pants out of my closet. If I do not take them out of the house and donate them, they have a way of returning to my closet, like when I run out of clean clothes. So, we need to remind ourselves often of our new belief until it's firmly engraved in our subconscious. Your old belief is unconsciously competent to control your life.

Your new belief is consciously incompetent, or

Your new belief is consciously competent.

You need to bring it to unconsciously competent by repetition.

Research shows that it takes taxi drivers and piano players some 10,000 hours of practice to become unconsciously competent. A child, before ever driving, is unconsciously incompetent – he thinks he knows how to drive. When a teenager is learning to drive, he is consciously incompetent – he knows he doesn't know. Once he has his driver's license, and for some time thereafter, he is consciously competent – it takes thinking to do some of the driving. Only after a long time spent driving and only some drivers become unconsciously competent – they can talk, eat, listen to music, scratch their head, and still drive safely. That is one reason that women in the old days were considered "bad drivers". They did occasional driving, not reaching the unconsciously competent state.

That is why using reminder notes, affirmations, and visual reminders as posters are so important and why they work.

This is also why it is important to pay attention to the music, books, and TV that we consume. If you choose to have a relationship, do not listen to music about heartbreak. Listen to music that people choose for their wedding songs that talk about upholding one other and being together. A good friend of mine has a saying: look where you are driving, don't drive where you are looking. That means keep your eyes on your target and go there!

26

GRATITUDE

All things, thoughts and emotions included, are energy. When we vibrate at the level of shame, regret, jealousy, fear, despair, blame and envy, we are in such a low vibration as to invite sickness, aging, and more of that same vibration. There is a saying: "I was so ashamed, I wanted the earth to open and swallow me." That is because the energy of shame is as low as the energy of a dying person.

When we vibrate at the level of gratitude, love, prayers, and blessings, we vibrate at a very high level where disease can't exist. It is like this: if you smile, even if you do not mean it, you can't be angry. You are smiling or angry, blaming or in gratitude, loving or in fear.

What if you can be grateful for the sun, the rain and the snow; for the ability to walk, to talk and to breathe? Can you be thankful for what you'd like to have and for what you do have?

Low vibration invites more of itself. The same is true about high vibration. The more thankful you are, the more things there will be to be thankful for.

I'm grateful for people cutting me off on the highway and slowing me down and saving me from an accident or a speeding ticket. I'm thankful for breathing and do not take it for granted. I know the pain of not being able to breathe. I'm thankful for my body that has taken in and safely stored my hurts. I'm thankful for my family and for my friends, for my teachers and students, and for my clients. I'm thankful for the birds that come to eat at my window. I'm thankful for you, reading these words now. There is so much more to be grateful for. <u>What are you grateful for? Can you find an additional 5 things to give thanks for?</u>

Recently, we learned of some radioactive water being dumped into the oceans in Japan and the concern of it reaching across the ocean to the American coast. Scientists assured the public that the amount is so small, there is no reason to panic. However, if we had 10 or 100 or 1000 sources of radioactive water leaking into the oceans, we would all start glowing, not just the fish. That is, if we are lucky enough to survive. I mean, the entire human race would disappear or change in way we can't imagine. A large enough radioactive spill would affect all living things and literally change the face of the earth. That is how awesome our actions are.

This illustrates three points:

We are all interconnected.

Our actions, thoughts, and feelings have influence things beyond our sight.

When we come together, we are formidable force for distraction or for creation.

What if our personal vibration was like that spill in Japan? Each of us contributes to the ocean of life. We each are a minute spring. When we choose to live and vibrate at the level of love, gratitude, and peace, we raise the collective vibration. One small flow of high vibration will be lost in the sea of fear, hate, and violence, but multiply that spark of high vibration 10, 100, 1000 or 1,000,000,000 fold and you have a current that is hot enough to melt the glaciers, or cold enough to freeze the oceans. It is said that the vibration of 100 highly-evolved beings is enough to balance and keep in check the negativity of the rest of the human race. What if we joined those 100 beings and started contributing to the high vibration? What world would we live in then? Just imagine!

World War II, with the immense distraction and the rebuilding thereafter, is another example of our collective power. Who would we be if we experienced the hunger of the hungry, the pain of the sick, and the longing of the children for the comfort of their mother's arms? What would we do if the only way to feel well was to heal the wounded? What would it take to have no fear, no abuse, no pollution, no wars, no poverty, and no sickness?

How would the world look if we stopped trying to fit into the impossible standards of the few? Who would we be if we lived in peace with our bodies, our talents, and our environment? Who would we be if shelter, food, peace, and creative expression were considered as basic human rights and were guaranteed to all? What if the creative ideas of all persons were considered, not just the ones who get funding? How much more wonderful technology would we have? Just imagine!

PART IV

This is a little book by design. It is a gift for you. I give you tools I gathered for a better life. They are your tools now. I hope you use them regularly and enjoy the process of self-discovery it may lead you through. If you find that you already know and practice most of these tools, do not be disappointed. Congratulate yourself for the high vibration you contribute to all humanity. Thank you.

Many of my clients find one of these tools enough to create a change in their life. Start with one tool that talks to you and master it, then move to another. What world would you create with these tools? I am truly excited to be your witness!

28

PRACTICE, PRACTICE, PRACTICE

What if you lived your life as an ongoing prayer or meditation?

What if you chant, "Trust", in your head while doing the dishes or shopping?

What if every time something happens you ask yourself: "What other possibilities are there?"

And when things seem stuck you ask, "What is the benefit in this that I choose not to see?"

What if you stop yourself, even in the middle of a sentence and do not use excuses, justifications, and buts?

What will it take for you to be willing to sit with the truth? Are you willing to know the truth? Are you willing to see the truth of you, of the other, and of the situation? Can you be with what is and not go into judgment?

Can you be in awe and gratitude, even when reality is not a perfect match to the image you created in your head? Can you be grateful for the small things in life, for being alive?

How would your actions be different if you ask yourself "What would love do?" before you think, say, or do anything?

What if instead of seeing others as the opposing team, you saw all people and things as members of your team?

Here is a creative mantra. You can add to it as it pleases you: I'm divine, I'm unconditional love, I'm truth, I'm creativity, I'm power, I'm control, I'm harmony, and everything is in divine order.

Just reading this book has raised your vibration! How can it get even better? What possibilities are there if you use this knowledge and live by it?

May your power be with you, and may you use it with love for the God/good of all!

Thank you, my friend. Be blessed!

THE BEGINNING!

ABOUT THE AUTHOR

Born in Bulgaria, Purim King immigrated to Israel as a teenager, where she learned a new language and served in the Israeli Army. She met and married an American and moved to NY, USA. After raising her two children, at age 44, she embarked on her healing journey. She graduated from a four-year program at Barbara Brennan School of Healing, followed by a two-year program of the Hakomi Institute. She then received her Bachelor of Science from SUNY Empire State College and her Master of Social Work from Adelphi University, becoming Licensed Clinical Social Worker in NY and Connecticut.

Purim is a teacher, master healer and holistic therapist, artist and a channel. She founded Core Wellness, providing trainings and direct care here and abroad. This is Purim's first book. Even though she says that she can't spell in any language, in her twenties she served as columnist for local newspaper in Jerusalem, Israel and she has written poems in Hebrew and English, over the years.

Purim aspires to be known as the kiss that made it better. She would like to see the principles taught presented in schools around the world, so that as a whole, we stop hitting our heads against the wall.

Made in the USA
Middletown, DE
30 August 2017